Ramsey

A COLLECTION OF IMAGES THROUGH THE YEARS

SUE WOOLLEY · MILES COWSILL

Published by:

Lily Publications, PO Box 33, Ramsey, Isle of Man IM99 4LP

Tel: +44 (0) 1624 898446   Fax: +44 (0) 1624 898449

E-mail: info@lilypublications.co.uk   Website: www.lilypublications.co.uk

Ramsey

A COLLECTION OF IMAGES THROUGH THE YEARS

Mooragh Park, Ramsey.

Produced and designed by Lily Publications Ltd 2013

PO Box 33, Ramsey, Isle of Man, British Isles, IM99 4LP.

Tel: +44 (0) 1624 898446   Fax: +44 (0) 1624 898449

www.lilypublications.co.uk   e-mail: info@lilypublications.co.uk

INTRODUCTION

Ramsey town, Ramsey town, shining by the sea …..

This new book on Ramsey follows the success of our series of books *Those Were the Days* which we have published during the last two years. This publication follows numerous requests to produce an historical picture book of Ramsey, together with some modern views of the town, as a souvenir book. The book does not set out to be a detailed history but an overview of this pretty coastal town which was visited by Queen Victoria and Prince Albert in 1847 and which later was to have the accolade of Royal Ramsey.

Ramsey, the second largest town on the Isle of Man, is blessed with a wonderful setting: cradled by the 10-mile sweep of the crescent bay, whose sandy shoreline extends to the northernmost Point of Ayre, against the backdrop of the high hills of North Barrule.

The name Ramsey was given by the Vikings and was first recorded in the *Chronicles of Man and the Isles* in the 14th century. Yet there are no buildings of great antiquity in Ramsey other than Ballure Church. The Burial Register dates from 1611 and in 1637 the building was reported to be in a near ruinous state. At various times over the years it has been restored.

The probable reason for Ramsey's lack of old buildings is that it suffered much turmoil throughout its early history.

Ramsey Harbour at low-tide - long before containers were invented.

Olaf, King of Mann, was murdered by his nephew Reginald near the harbour in 1154. Somerled, the 12th-century Thane of Argyll, made a historic landing here, and a century later Robert the Bruce passed through on his way to besiege Castle Rushen.

Centuries on, landing in Ramsey became a lot easier when the magnificent Queen's Pier was built in 1886. Thrusting out into deep water for a distance of 2,248 feet, it established Ramsey as a popular stopping-off point for steamers en route to other ports of call. Today Ramsey harbour, with its twin forcep-like breakwaters at the entrance, offers shelter to yachts, coasters and trawlers.

Another very distinctive feature of Ramsey's harbour is the iron swing bridge, 225 feet long, which came into operation in 1892. On the landward side of the bridge is Ramsey shipyard, which constructed one of the world's first iron ships as well as the *Star of India*, now displayed as an attraction in the American port of San Diego. The yard also built the world's first two ships specifically designed as oil tankers.

Flowing into the bay via the harbour is the Island's longest river, the Sulby. In fact, Ramsey was once an island. In 1630 the town was virtually destroyed by the sea, a continuous threat until the early years of the 19th century.

In 1881, Mooragh Park was created on reclaimed wasteland, protected by a new promenade and sea wall. It is a very popular spot and a great attraction for all ages, with 40 acres of gardens and a 12-acre boating lake. Canoeing, sailing and other water-based activities are part of the draw, as are the summer concerts and galas held in the park and the Lakeside Centre.

Today, Ramsey has a population of around 7,400 residents and is an important and commercial shopping centre for those living in the north of the Island. Trade continues to prosper between the UK and Ramsey with the services of Mezeron and the Ramsey Steamship Company. The port remains an important centre for fishing, especially for the Manx delicacy of Queenies collected from the shores around the Island. Holidaymakers from all over the world continue to come to the town, especially during TT and the Manx Grand Prix, for enthusiasts to get iconic views of the riders in Parliament Square.

The authors have sourced from various parties a wealth of historical views and many of the pictures have come from the Keig collection acquired by Lily Publications in 2012. Most of the modern views of the town were taken by Tony Lloyd Davies, who has produced a variety of pictures with a different eye perspective of the town.

We are grateful to Michael Kinrade for his input to the book with historical material and photographs, pending his new book in 2014 on 'Parliament Street' which he has been researching for many years. Our thanks go to the newly opened Ramsey Heritage Centre Committee, Quayle's Hall in Albert Street for all their help and encouragement with this book. Finally, we are grateful to Stan Basnett, Richard Davis, Ronnie Corkish, Les Clarke, Tony Harmer, Richard Kirkman, Nicola Green, Manx National Heritage and Charles Guard of the Manx Heritage Foundation for their assistance with the book. Constance Radcliffe's iconic book *Shining by the Sea* is also acknowledged.

Sue Woolley and Miles Cowsill
November 2013

This photograph shows 12 of the 13 men who made up the first Fire Brigade to be formed in Ramsey in 1887. Also depicted are examples of the type of equipment in use at the time, such as standpipes and the long copper branches or nozzles.

The HMY **Victoria** and **Albert** anchored in Ramsey Bay during the royal visit of King George V and Queen Mary. This was the third yacht to be named Victoria and Albert and she served four sovereigns, and was decommissioned as royal yacht in 1939.

Left: Crowds on the seafront at Ramsey watch the launch of the **Mary Isabella** during a training exercise. The lifeboat in Ramsey has always played an important role in the town.

Above: Mona Street, possibly 1895 after the 'Big Snow'. Note the Billiards Hall on the right.

An early view of Ramsey, with the area which later became the Mooragh Park, opened in 1887. The Sulby River discharged to the sea here until North Shore Road and the Mooragh Promenade enclosed the area. From the dress of the people in the picture it could well be dated in the 1870s. On the right are some of the buildings at the shipyard which provided major employment for the town. On the left are the North and South Piers, built to provide a sheltered passageway into the harbourside. At the end of the South Pier stands the Lifeboat House, built in 1869. Against the harbour wall a Steam Packet paddle steamer can be seen. It has two funnels set close together with the first just in line with the front of the paddlebox; it could therefore be **Douglas (II)**, *which was in service between 1864 and 1889.*

An early Edwardian view taken below Albert Tower looking over Ramsey with the Queen's Pier and harbour entrance.

The Fleetwood Steamer **Cevic** ran aground near Port Lewaigue, Maughold in 1927. The skipper and the crew were all rescued but the vessel was a total loss. Wreckage of the former trawler can still be seen today at low tide.

A postcard of Mooragh Park illustrates that there have been very few changes made in this popular area of the town over the years since it was established in 1887.

A view looking up Parliament Street taken in the Edwardian period shows iron railings to the left which were removed in 1962.

The Palace at Ramsey was originally built in the early 1890s as the Palace Concert Hall and Ballroom. It was later substantially modernised and renamed the Plaza. It closed in 1974 and was demolished completely in 1990.

The 'old' Town Hall, built in 1888/9, was a handsome building that also housed the Fire Brigade. It was demolished in 1971. Its successor, never popular with the public, was demolished in 2000. The present town hall was designed by architect Gordon Clarke; built by McArds and opened in April 2002.

Ramsey Fire Brigade pictured outside the Town Hall with their new Merryweather 30 hp appliance, which was the second motor-driven appliance to arrive on the Island. It was named Richdale after the Chairman of the Town Commissioners, Mr J N Richdale, who is in the centre of the photograph on the front row with Mr J Smith, the Fire Brigade's Chief Officer.

Ramsey has been part of the TT for more than 100 years, starting in 1911 when the race was held for the very first time on the famous 37.73mile Mountain Circuit. The Senior race that year was won by Oliver Godfrey on an 'Indian' machine, with an average speed of 47.63mph. Compare that with the 2013 event when the Senior race was won by John McGuinness riding a Honda, with an average of 128.94mph. Ramsey has several incomparable vantage points for the fans. The bikes speed into town along Lezayre Road, slowing down to negotiate Parliament Square, accelerate towards Cruickshank's Corner and on up to round the sharp left hand bend at the Hairpin. The climb continues to Waterworks and Gooseneck and then its full throttle as they head towards the Mountain Mile and the Bungalow.... Above left: 'Ginger' Wood enjoys the foreground on his Jawa during the 1935 TT, whilst Ramsey Town Hall occupies the background in Parliament Square, and above right: In this photograph from 1912 the rider on the right uses the footpath to avoid the worst holes in the road on the approach to Cruickshanks.

Right: Ramsey Primitive Methodist Chapel was completed in 1892, but was only used for about fifty years. The site is now occupied by Millichaps' home furnishers.

Below: This picture from the Keig Collection shows the current site of the Roman Catholic Church after the buildings around it were demolished to make way for the new church which was completed during 1910. The inset view shows the church under construction during the winter period of 1910. The church design was the early work of Giles Gilbert Scott.

Right: This wonderful Edwardian view takes in the seafront at Ramsey. The Bowling and Billards Saloon can be seen on the present site of the Sure Strike Bowling and Leisure Centre.

Below: Part of people's holiday experience of coming to the north of the Island and Ramsey was to enjoy a trip up the Sulby River. This postcard shows a variety of boats at Sulby with holidaymakers enjoying the countryside.

Bathing huts on Ballure beach. The boarding houses above left were later developed as the Beach Hotel and more recently as the Fountains private apartments.

Guest houses at the top of Ballure Road, on the approach to Ramsey via the coast road. Most are now private homes, but some, like Thorncliff, still take in visitors.

Preparing for Christmas: Kermeen's butcher shop in Peel Street.

King George V and Queen Mary make their way down Ramsey Pier after their visit to the town during 1920.

As part of the royal visit to Ramsey in 1920, four special cars were brought over to the Island to assist the royal party. This picture shows the cars outside the gasworks with the eight chauffeurs of the royal party.

This interesting view shows Ramsey in the early Twenties prior to the extensive development of the town. The photo takes in the former church of Ballure now a private home, which is now surrounded by properties built during the sixties.

A view of Ramsey Pier with scouts making their way down from the town to await the Steam Packet ship back to England.

Local residents look on as an enthusiastic Edwardian swimmer dives into the open-air swimming baths at Ramsey.

The swing bridge in Ramsey was built in 1892 and still dominates the town today as a distinctive feature. This Edwardian postcard shows holidaymakers and residents waiting for the bridge to reopen after allowing a boat through to the inner harbour.

*'**Cloud of Iona**' amphibian aircraft used for pleasure flights between Glasgow and Belfast and the Isle of Man. The plane is pictured here on the beach at Ramsey in the early 1930s.*

The bus station in Ramsey was built in the late twenties and still remains today as an important terminus for buses from Douglas and Peel.

Queen's Pier was used by thousands of people between 1886, when it opened, to 1970 when it closed to passenger vessels. It has been closed completely since 1991 and its future remains uncertain despite a recent government survey showing that a clear majority of the Island's public were in favour of saving the landmark.

Right: *This interesting view, provided by Raymotors, shows on the left the former cinema of the town before the car dealers redeveloped the site. The view takes in the early development of Brookfield Avenue. Note that the road from the entrance to Brookfield Avenue remains in an uncompleted state.*

Below: *An aerial view of Ramsey showing Queen's Court and King's Court apartment blocks, which were built in the Sixties by Malcolm Milton in partnership with Ramsey Town Commissioners as part of the South Ramsey re-development scheme.*

ALBERT TOWER & 'ROYAL RAMSEY'

Another view of King George V and Queen Mary on a walk around the town meeting children and residents. Such was the enthusiasm on this visit of the Royal family that people can be viewed on the rooftops of the shops – something that could never be considered today in the world of Health & Safety.

Albert Tower, the town's most iconic landmark, commemorates the royal visit of 20th September, 1847 when the royal yacht, en route from Scotland with Queen Victoria and the Prince Consort on board, anchored in Ramsey Bay.

While Her Majesty stayed at sea, Prince Albert came ashore and enjoyed a stroll through Ballure Glen to the top of Lhergy Frissell, accompanied by a small party of dignitaries and a guide, who according to local history was a local barber. On reaching the summit, the Prince was deeply impressed by the sweeping panorama. Soon after this visit, the townspeople decided that a tower should be erected on the site of where the royal feet had stood. On Easter Monday the following year the foundation stone was laid in the presence of a very large crowd. Beneath the stone was placed a bottle containing an inscription in Manx and English commemorating the event.

The tower, constructed of Claughbane slate with cornerstones of South Barrule granite, was officially opened on 24th July, 1849. Despite the 'exceedingly unfavourable' weather, 2,000 people attended the ceremony. Albert Tower holds a special place in Ramsey's affections and its image is incorporated into the town crest.

Royal Visits

'Royal Ramsey' acquired its name because, in the days before air travel, it was the starting point of three royal visits to the Island - in 1847, 1902 and 1920. The first was that of Queen Victoria and Prince Albert in 1847, followed by King Edward VII and Queen Alexandra in 1902 and King George V and Queen Mary in 1920. More recently, the King and Queen of Norway were the first visitors to the new Town Hall on 6th July 2002.

Top left: *Her Royal Highness the Queen Mother inspects the Guard of Honour at Ramsey during her visit to the town on 4th July 1962.*

Top right: *King George V and Queen Mary talk to residents and nurses from the Cottage Hospital during their visit in 1920.*

Middle right: *Crowds throng King George VI and Queen Elizabeth when they visited Ramsey following the end of the Second World War.*

Above right: *Her Majesty Queen Elizabeth II with the Mayor of Ramsey, Beryl Quine talks to the crowds in Market Place on 8th August 1989.*

Above left: *Another view of Her Majesty Queen Elizabeth II with Prince Philip accepting flowers from a resident of the town in 1955.*

(All photos Ramsey Town Commissioners Archives)

MILNTOWN

MiIntown, one of Ramsey's finest houses, was home to the Christians, the Island's most powerful family, for 600 years. William Christian (Illiam Dhone), one of the most dramatic figures in Manx history, was born and raised there.

Illiam Dhone became a legendary figure because of the part he played during the time of the English Civil War. He started out as a close confidant of the 7th Earl of Derby (Yn Stanlagh Mooar) and held the high office of Receiver, but all that was to change….

When the Earl left the Island in 1651 to join the Royalist forces, he left Christian in charge of the Island militia, and committed his countess, Charlotte de la Tremoille to his care.

The Countess, on learning that her husband was imprisoned in England, made proposals for the surrender of the Island to the Parliamentary forces in return for his life.

A turn of the century view of Milntown. The estate at the time extended to almost 500 acres reaching as far north as the railway line and as far east as Ramsey.

A view of Milntown taken in the early 20th century with sheep grazing on the grounds. Today this view could not be taken as the trees have grown much higher and further trees and shrubs have been planted.

But the insular militia, not trusting the terms of her proposals, rose up under Christian's command and successfully negotiated its own terms. The Countess and her children were banished from the Island. The Earl, meanwhile, was beheaded at Bolton.

Following the Restoration, Charles, 8th Earl of Derby, succeeded as Lord of Mann. Angry at Christian's role in his family's losses during the Civil War, he ordered his arrest for treason. Christian was unfairly tried and executed by firing squad at Hango Hill, Castletown on 2nd January 1663. A pardon from the King, Charles II, arrived too late.

The Manx proclaimed Christian a martyr and annually commemorate the anniversary of his execution.

The Christian dynasty died out in 1918 and Milntown passed through several ownerships. The last owner, Sir Clive Edwards, died in 1999, bequeathing the estate to a private charitable trust, with the directive that it be used for the benefit of the public. The trustees embarked on a development plan and the house and grounds are now open for everyone to enjoy.

THE GIBBS OF THE GROVE

A visit to The Grove Rural Life Museum on the outskirts of Ramsey is like stepping back in time to a vanished way of life. The house is an early Victorian villa, built in 1840 as a holiday home for Duncan Gibb, a wealthy Liverpool shipping merchant, and his family. He also acquired several acres of farm land.

Mr Gibb retired to The Grove around 1862, but died just five years later, leaving his home occupied by his widow and other family members.

His only son, also named Duncan, died at the early age of 48 leaving a wife, two daughters and a son. It was his daughters, Janet and Alice, who came to live with their grandmother at The Grove and remained there for the rest of their lives, having made a promise that they would not leave, or get married, in order to continue to look after the house, the garden and the pony.

The sisters enjoyed a full and active social life until the outbreak of the First World War. From then on, their finances were stretched to the limits, but with unending resourcefulness and a strong commitment to their family home, they managed to carry on.

Ironically, it is because of their financially-restrained circumstances that the house remained virtually unchanged for a century, epitomising the way of life for Victorian gentlewomen.

The sisters were familiar figures in Ramsey and worshipped at St Paul's Church. Miss Alice died in 1971 aged 90 and Miss Janet three years later, shortly after her 96th birthday.

They bequeathed The Grove to the Manx Museum and it

A postcard from the Victorian era of the Grove. Today the site is run by Manx National Heritage.

is beautifully maintained by Manx National Heritage for the public to enjoy.

The house may not be of great architectural importance, but the atmosphere gives the visitor a fascinating glimpse of upper middle class life in the Victorian era. The cobbled yard, outbuildings, vintage carriages and farm implements all add to the experience.

NEWSPAPER DAYS OF RAMSEY

The Ramsey Courier was a northern institution for almost a century. It was launched in 1884 by advocate John Craine, who ran it, with varying degrees of success, for five years. In 1890, the goodwill, copyright, and printing machinery were bought at auction by C.B. Heyes, chief reporter of the Isle of Man Times. He published the paper twice weekly, on Tuesdays and Fridays.

Like many local businesses, the Courier fell victim to the Dumbell's Bank Crash of 1900. Mr Heyes was compelled to put the business in the hands of a receiver and he moved to London to continue working in newspapers.

Shortly before this, Hugo Teare, a Ramsey man, had entered employment with Mr Heyes. Although only 23, Mr Teare had the courage to purchase the ailing newspaper and by diligent application put it back on its feet. In 1921 he was joined in management by his younger brother, Cecil Teare. Both brothers were prominent in public life and served as MHK's.

It remained in the Teare family until 1957 – a period of nearly 60 years. Shorter periods of ownership followed, Messrs. C.M. Watterson and later advocate J.J. Christian, before passing out of Manx hands in 1979.

One man synonymous with the Courier was veteran journalist Syd Boulton, who edited the paper for a number of years and whose long-running About People column showed his encyclopaedic knowledge of Ramsey and the north. Syd died in February 1983 aged 73 and is still remembered with great affection by many people in the town.

Printing works of the Ramsey Courier in 1934. Syd Boulton is in the centre, folding newspapers ready for distribution.

Ramsey Courier office and printing staff 1970. Left to right: Doreen McLean, Alan Bell, Brenda Garrett, Stuart Clements, Steph Callister, Cliffie Corkill, Peter McElroy, Brian Quirk, Crawford MacLaren, Roger Bagnall, Robbie Radcliffe; front: Syd Boulton, Sue Wood (Woolley), Ian Smith and Fred Quirk.

FISHING

In 1841, only two heads of households in the whole of Ramsey were described as 'fishermen'. By 1861 this number had risen to 15. In the spring, the boats sailed to Kinsale, south-east Ireland, for mackerel. From June to September, they followed the shoals of herring around the coast of the Isle of Man. From October to December, they fished for herring off Howth Head, Dublin. Their boats were 'nickeys', 'nobbies' and 'half-deckers'.

Occasional extremely large catches were recorded: in September 1849, for example, the Ramsey yacht 'Sam Weller' nearly sank under her load of skate.

In April 1852, a halibut weighing 1cwt 75lb was caught in the bay.

An early Keig picture taken of Ramsey Harbour with the traditional sailing barge leaving the port. Note the rowing boats in front of this picture which will have formed part of the holiday experience for visitors.

Local residents in Market Place inspect a wealth of fish caught over night.

Another view of fish on display in Market Square. This picture shows the original façade of St Paul's Square before the construction of the new buildings in the

The spring of 1859 saw immense shoals of mackerel observed near land.

1865 – 1914 was a golden age, with boats setting out in search of herring, mackerel, cod and salmon; oyster beds were established in the bay. When catches were plentiful, boys would be absent from school and could be found selling fish.

In 1890, Ramsey had 40 mackerel boats and 30 cod smacks. Cod was laid out for sale by auction near the 'fish steps' in the harbour corner nearest Market Place.

Families engaged in the fishing were the Looneys, Kaighens, Kinnins, Garretts, Gales, Kinrades, Kenyons, Corkishs and Stowells. They were later joined by country people with the surnames Christian, Brew, Camaish, Cannell, Crennell and Gawne. There were also fishermen named Ball, Binks, Crix, Godfrey, Graham, Greaves and Kneen.

Fishermen stand around the harbour at Ramsey waiting to inspect catches from the overnight fishing. The swing bridge in this picture had recently been completed

BRICKWORKS, GAS WORKS & OTHER INDUSTRIES

Brickworks

Immediately after the war, in 1946, a new light industry was set up in Ramsey to produce calcium silicate (sand lime) bricks, to meet the urgent demand for new housing on the Island.

Manx Bricks Ltd. was formed by a Manchester businessman, Mr J.H. Murray, who had retired to Ramsey the previous year, but soon launched into the manufacturing of bricks.

Mr W.A. Coffey, chairman of Ramsey Town Commissioners, was managing director and Mr Murray's son, Bill was appointed manager.

The 'Homestead Works' at Gardener's Lane, Milntown, with its 75 ft high chimney, was built by Messrs. Sutcliffe Speakman & Co. of Leigh, Lancashire.

At its peak, the brickworks employed 30 men and six women who worked a three-shift system to produce 290,000 bricks per week. 140 tons of salt-free sand from Kimmeragh, Bride and 10 tons of lime from Billown quarry in the south were supplied daily. Isle of Man Railways provided a siding at

*The Ramsey steamship vessel **Ben Rein** awaits her cargo with the gasworks behind her.*

A stoker emptying the retort at Ramsey Gas Works.

*This view shows the gasworks after its closure in a slightly dilapidated state prior to it being demolished. The steamer **J B Kee** is making ready to leave the port on the high tide.*

Holidaymakers enjoy the delights of boating on the 'Mooragh' during the height of one of the Edwardian holiday seasons. In the background the gasworks can be easily made out with North Barrule.

Milntown for the delivery of raw materials and the dispatch of bricks.

The bricks were pale in colour, strong, durable and fireproof, with clean cut edges and a smooth surface. They came in three grades, suitable for foundations, facing work and interiors.

In its short lifetime, Manx Bricks Ltd. produced over 55 million bricks to build hundreds of local authority houses at Seamount Road and Brookhill Road, Ramsey; Lambhill, Bride; Willaston and Pulrose estates, Douglas; Janet's Corner, Castletown, and private houses dotted around Ramsey.

By 1955 the building industry had gone into decline and the company ceased trading.

But that was not the end of the story - the brickworks were dismantled and sold to Peter Pan Tiles in Western Australia. The whole outfit – 450 tons of plant - was shipped to Freemantle. Around two dozen key workers, their wives and families went too. They included Mr R.B. Warburton (works manager), John McCormack, Mr W. Wilde, Herbert Coffey, Mr R. Cowle, Mr and Mrs Fred Cude and Dennis Cannell.

The 'Homestead Works' site was sold to the Manx Electricity Board and Ramsey Power Station was developed.

Clague's Foundry

There is plenty of evidence around the town of work produced at Clague's Foundry, which operated from premises between East Quay and Queen's Promenade from 1865 – 1913.

Manhole covers, garden gates and railings, gratings, even mangles, ploughs and WC cisterns were among the iron goods embossed with the name 'Clague's'.

Clague's manufactured railings, seats and lamp standards for the Queen's Pier. As well as delicate ornamental work, the foundry undertook heavy engineering work such as a trailer for the pier railway.

The drinking fountain in Market Place is another fine example. A more unusual item is the model of the right hand of the Sulby Giant, Arthur Caley, displayed in the Manx Museum.

The business was founded by John Clague, who had been foreman blacksmith at Laxey Mines. He bought the premises on East Quay and established the foundry as John Clague & Son Ltd. It comprised a moulding shop, steam-operated engine room, blacksmith's workshop, fitting and pattern shop and an office.

The 1889-90 record book showed around 18 employees, including eight apprentices. Wages were meagre and the total weekly wage bill did not exceed £13. Apprentices earned the grand sum of 7d per day.

In 1913, the premises was acquired by the Isle of Man Steam Packet Company and Clague's opened a shop at 39 Parliament Street. All foundry worked ceased.

The business continued in existence until 1964 when it was acquired by Gelling's Foundry Ltd. of Douglas.

Other Industries

As well as the brickworks, the salt works, shipbuilding and Clague's Foundry, other industries have long disappeared, such as breweries, sawmills, tanneries, 'pop' works, smithies, dairies, coachbuilders and saddlers. Some readers may have worked at the Aristoc Nylon Factory on Gladstone Park or at the jeans factory in the present Masonic Hall, Lezayre Road – two industries that once employed a significant number of workers and played an important role in the economy of the town. At least we still have Ramsey Bakery, which celebrated its 40th anniversary in 2012.

Clague's Foundry on East Quay was demolished in 1915. Look carefully and you will see a lady in the doorway on the right and some workmen on the roof.

In this photograph two of J. Monk's steam coasters are loading gravel at the Point of Ayre for work on the dock extensions at Liverpool with J.B. Kee acting as agent in his own right.

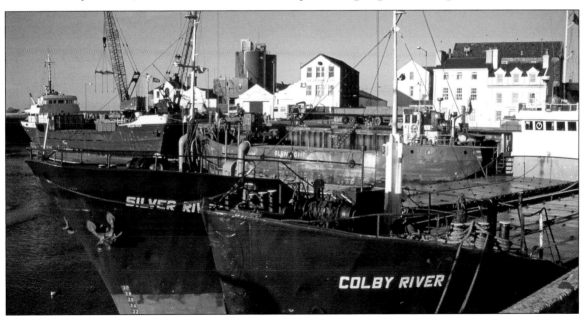

*Both Mezeron and the Ramsey Steamship Company have used the harbour facilities at Ramsey for many years. The introduction of larger tonnage and the **Ben-my-Chree** in 1998 has seen a decline in the use of the port in recent years. This view, taken by Stan Basnett, takes in a busy harbour view with Mezeron's **Greeba River**, **Silver River** and **Colby River** in the Seventies. (Stan Basnett)*

STEAM PACKET

At the turn of the century the Isle of Man Steam Packet was operating a fleet of eleven vessels, which comprised of eight paddle-steamers and three twin-screw steamers. The company was to make a major impact on the Manx holiday industry during the early 20th century with the expansion of services to and from the Island. As the Isle of Man became more popular with holidaymakers, especially from the North-West, not only did the fleet expand but the vessels became larger to accommodate the popularity of the Island.

The company played an important role during the First and Second World Wars with their vessels and by the end of the Second World War extensive rebuilding and refurbishment of the fleet had to take place for the twilight years of the holiday industry, which was to change radically during the early Sixties with the advent of package holidays to Spain.

As part of the extensive web of operations of the Isle of Man Steam Packet Company, which concentrated the majority of their operations into Douglas, the Ramsey operations were also important with services to Belfast, Ardrossan, Fleetwood, Whitehaven and Liverpool. With the tidal restrictions of Ramsey and the building of the Queen's Pier in 1886, the latter became important for a regular operation of the company.

With the demise of the holiday industry, the Isle of Man Steam Packet Company reduced its operations during the late Fifties and Sixties, and eventually the Ramsey service was closed by the company on 10th September 1970 with the *Manxman* making the last visit to the pier from Belfast.

To support their operations in the first half of the 20th century, the Steam Packet produced a wide variety of brochures to attract holidaymakers to the Island.

*A splendid study of the **Snaefell** (2) rolling in a stiff breeze as she leaves Ramsey and still flying the 'Blue Peter' from her foremast. The ship is full of the volunteers on their way back to the UK after their annual camp at Milntown. (Stan Basnett Collection)*

Below: Passengers load the **Viking** at Ramsey pier. *(Stan Basnett Collection)*

Right: The paddle steam **Mona's Queen** seen arriving at Ramsey pier. *(Ferry Publications Library)*

Bottom left: Alongside at Ramsey the Isle of Man Steam Packet steamer **Peveril** attracts a good crowd of sightseers pending her departure. *(Stan Basnett Collection)*

Bottom right: The double-ended **Mona** is seen leaving Ramsey with a full load of passengers on a high tide. *(Stan Basnett Collection)*

Right: The much-loved **Lady of Mann** (2) berthing at Queen's Pier, Ramsey on passage from Belfast on 14th July 1968. (Stan Basnett)

Below: The **Mona's Isle** (5) berthing at Queen's Pier, Ramsey en route from Belfast to Douglas on 21st July 1968. (Stan Basnett)

Below right: A wonderful view of the **Fenella** (3) turning in the harbour at Ramsey on her last sailing into the port from Lioverpool. (Stan Basnett)

ELLAN VANNIN TRAGEDY

The Isle of Man Steam Packet vessel Ellan Vannin, carrying 14 passengers and 21 crew, sank at the mouth of the river Mersey on 3rd December, 1909, with the loss of all on board.

She had left Ramsey harbour at 1.13am that day, bound for Liverpool, under the command of Captain James Teare, an able and experienced navigator. She was carrying mail and 60 tonnes of cargo, including sheep and oats.

There was a stiff breeze as the ship left harbour, but no worse than was frequently experienced on winter sailings. Conditions worsened, however, and by 6.35am, when the ship arrived at the Mersey bar light-ship, the wind had risen to almost hurricane force 11 with high waves exceeding 20ft (6.1m).

To this day, no-one knows exactly what happened, but it seems probable that waves overwhelmed the ship and she foundered.

The Island was plunged into mourning and a Disaster Fund was set up to assist the bereaved families.

An official enquiry concluded that the Ellan Vannin sank as a result of heavy seas.

A plaque commemorating the tragedy can be seen near the harbour steps on West Quay, close to where the ship departed on her final voyage.

No Isle of Man Steam Packet Company vessel has been named Ellan Vannin since.

'The Ellan Vannin Tragedy' made famous by the Liverpool folk group The Spinners commemorates the event:

> *Snaefell, Tynwald, Ben my Chree*
> *Fourteen ships had sailed the sea*
> *Proudly bearing a Manx name*
> *But there's one will never again*
> *Oh Ellan Vannin of the Isle of Man Company*
> *Oh Ellan Vannin, lost in the Irish Sea...*

*Another view of ill-fated **Ellan Vannin** leaving Ramsey. The vessel was built as the **Mona's Isle** in 1860.*

*The plaque in memory of **Ellan Vannin** on the quayside at Ramsey..*

*A very rare view of the **Ellan Vannin** arriving at Ramsey on a cargo run from north-west England.*

RAMSEY STEAMSHIP COMPANY

For 100 years, the 'Ben boats' have been synonymous with Ramsey. They are the 'trademark' of the Ramsey Steamship Company, which was founded in April 1913 by Captain John Brown (J.B.) Kee.

'J.B.' was educated at the Old Grammar School, Ramsey and followed his father into a career at sea.

When he returned to shore he settled down to business life in the town. His father, Captain J.T. Kee, after a long career as a master mariner, had established a coal merchants' business on West Quay and his son joined him in the venture.

Together they conceived the idea of owning a steamship that would bring in coal and other bulk cargoes to the Island at more competitive rates for other traders.

Their first ship was named the *Ben Veg* (Little Woman). The company grew and developed and new vessels were acquired, each being given a Manx name with the prefix 'Ben'. The list includes *Ben Ain, Ben Ellan, Ben Maye, Ben Rein, Ben Seyr, Ben Vane, Ben Varrey, Ben Veen, Ben Veg* and *Ben Vooar*. For the past one hundred years, the Ben boats have been synonymous with the port of Ramsey.

The company's history is very much entwined with that of the Kee family. Its co-founder, Captain John Thomas Kee (1854-1926) was the son of a Ramsey blacksmith. He did not follow his father's trade, but went to sea and rose to be a ship's Master.

After a long and adventurous career at sea, he returned to shore and established a coal merchant's business on West Quay. His son John Brown Kee (1883-1934) joined him in the venture.

It was a natural development of their enterprise that in the process of importing large quantities of coal they began to consider the advantages of owning their own steamer to bring in cargoes at more favourable rates.

Accordingly, they assembled a group of Ramsey businessmen with the object of acquiring one or more small steamships to trade between the Isle of Man, chiefly Ramsey, and ports on the mainland.

Those involved in the scheme were Frederick Brew (banker), Thomas Baker Cowley (corn merchant), John William Hyde (advocate), and Robert Evan Kennish (corn merchant).

The proposed venture attracted considerable local support and on 19th May, 1913, the Ramsey Steamship Co. Ltd. came into being, Robert Brew as Chairman, John Brown Kee as Secretary and Manager.

Garston to Ramsey was quoted at four shillings to four shillings and threepence per ton which, the prospectus claimed, allows for a drop to 3/6 on 150 tons per trip.

It was agreed that trading would be limited to the north Irish Sea, between Londonderry and the River Clyde as a northern boundary, and between Bardsey Island in Wales and Arklow on the east coast of Ireland as a southern boundary.

A completely new vessel was built to order by the Larne Shipbuilding Company, Northern Ireland, at a cost of £4,089. The new ship was a coaster of 159 gross tonnage, captained by John Cowley and named *Ben Veg*.

The *Ben Veg*'s maiden voyage was on the 17th August 1914 when she carried a cargo of stone to Liverpool. Other bulk cargoes of sand, cement, salt and, of course, coal were

Right: Cargo being unloaded on the quay at Ramsey during the early twenties. (Ramsey Steamship Co.)

*Below: The coaster the **Ben Vooar** ('big woman') seen here at her home port of Ramsey at low tide. (Ramsey Steamship Co.)*

*Right: A Midwood photograph of the **Ben Varrey** (1) taken from the south pier at Ramsey. Judging by her position she appears to be dodging, waiting for the tide to make before entering harbour. (T.H. Midwood – John Cowley collection)*

*Below: The **Ben Veen** awaiting further cargo at Ramsey. (Stan Basnett collection)*

*The **Ben Veg** (2) underwent repairs at Ramsey shipyard. (Stan Basnett)*

soon forthcoming, so that at the first AGM on the company in October 1914 held at Corlett's Tea Rooms, Ramsey, the mood was celebratory.

Throughout the past one hundred years, which has seen two World Wars, post-war Depressions and the transition from steam to engine power, the company has sustained a steady course, remaining a genuinely independent undertaking and enjoying a high reputation.

SHOPPING STORIES

Moughtin Brothers delicatessen in Bourne Place was a part of the Ramsey street-scene for 37 years, from 1975 to 2012 when the proprietors Kim and Mark Moughtin retired. The brothers were brought up in the retail trade. Their father, Gerald, was proprietor of Aldis & Moughtin, a high class grocery store at 14 Parliament Street (currently Costa Coffee). At the time, it was in the vanguard of changing culinary tastes, being one of the first grocers in the Island to import Continental meats and cheeses. Kim joined the business straight from school in 1967 and Mark two years later. When their father retired in 1972, the brothers stayed on as managers under the new owner, James Kissack Ltd. Three years later they set up in business together as Moughtin Brothers in the Bourne Place premises formerly occupied by Brew the butchers and more latterly by George Kelly, butcher.

Customers came on a regular basis from all over the Island to buy brands of fine fare not generally available locally and for the old fashioned service no longer found elsewhere. Sadly the shutters came down for the last time at 5pm on Saturday, 26th May 2012.

One of the most iconic properties in the town is Saddle Buildings. One day in August 1955 there was an outbreak of fire within Saddle Buildings. A bedroom on the top floor was alight, with smoke and flames coming out of the windows attracting a large crowd of onlookers.

Something which is unimaginable now was that, as the fire raged in the bedroom and the fire brigade were tackling it, singing and dancing carried on in the bar below. The licensee had refused to close because the place was "thronged with visitors and people were enjoying themselves".

Another story concerns 20 Parliament Street, where the Isle of Man Bank is now. The Ramsey Courier on 15th May, 1936 reported the following: 'A sequel to a shop improvement scheme was heard in the Ramsey High Court, when Mona Clayton, of 20 Parliament Street sued Corkhill & Callow, builders and contractors, for £20. Mr Eason appeared for the plaintiff and Mr Teare for the defendants.'

Mr Eason said that while the defendants were carrying out business operations at Messrs. Lays' premises in Parliament Street, the wall was broken through and damage was caused to the contents of a drawing room in the house occupied by the plaintiff.

Mr Teare's defence was on the question of damage caused. He tendered a certain sum, which had been paid into court.

The plaintiff said she occupied six rooms at 20 Parliament Street. Between the hours of 3pm and 5pm on 30th January she was at the trade exhibition at the Swimming Pool Ballroom. On her return she found a huge hole in the wall, 'big enough to push a small barrow through'. There were large stones on the floor and white plaster adhering to everything. There was nobody in the house at the time. All her best things were in the room. All her possessions were covered in a white chalk and not even a suction sweeper would remove it. She informed Mr Callow next morning and he came to see the damage – three weeks later.

Mrs Clayton was seeking damages for items of clothing, which she valued at £17.12s.5d. Mr Teare disputed this, saying the plaintiff could not possibly afford such clothes as she was in receipt of poor relief. Mrs Clayton replied that the clothes were a gift from her daughter.

The presiding deemster thought it would have been better if independent evidence had been called to show the state of the room immediately after the incident. He felt the damages claimed were slightly exaggerated, yet the damages suggested by the defendants of £1 were too low. He gave judgment in favour of the plaintiff for £5, plus costs.

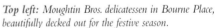

Top left: *Moughtin Bros. delicatessen in Bourne Place, beautifully decked out for the festive season.*

Top right & above: *W. Brown, Family Grocer and Wine Merchant, occupied, 14 Parliament Street, later home to Aldis & Moughtin, Ramsey Art Gallery and currently Costa Coffee. Brown's was obviously well-established enough to produce its own blend of tea. Other picture shows the interior of Brown's with lots of tinned goods and flitches of bacon hanging from hooks in the ceiling.*

Left: *Jas. Lay's gent's outfitters, a branch of the Douglas firm, served the town for many years. It is now the popular gift shop, The Tide.*

45

RAMSEY COTTAGE HOSPITAL

A true jewel: small in size but of enormous value. The foundation stone of Ramsey Cottage Hospital was laid on 26th June, 1906 and the opening ceremony took place on 23rd July the following year.

The need for a hospital in the north was poignantly illustrated in January 1904 when Lindsay Anderson, the eight year old son of Mr and Mrs D.E. Anderson of Ballaugh died on the way to Noble's Hospital in Douglas suffering from acute appendicitis. His grieving parents approached High Bailiff Cruickshank of Ramsey, who in turn applied to the Trustees of the Henry Bloom Noble estate for financial assistance in establishing a hospital to serve the north.

The trustees granted £6,000 to purchase one and a half acres at Ballachrink, Lezayre, a spacious, green field plot within the town boundary, and on it to erect and furnish a cottage hospital.

The Trustees of the estate of Pierre Baume, a wealthy Douglas recluse, donated £1,000 to establish an Endowment Fund, which was then and later augmented by many local people including Mr and Mrs Anderson.

The blue stone principally used in the construction of the hospital came from the Starch Mills Quarry, Sulby Glen, with quoins of St Bee's sandstone cut by Ramsey stonemason, Edward Christian. The building contractors were Messrs. Jas. Callow & Sons and the plumbing and gas fitting was carried out by Mr F.W. Callow.

Extensions have been added and improvements carried out over the years as Ramsey Cottage Hospital has kept pace with medical developments.

The centenary in 1997 was celebrated with a series of

The opening ceremony of Ramsey Cottage Hospital on 23rd July 1907 was attended by many Ramsey residents on a scorching hot day. Note in this picture the parasols and umbrellas over the ladies' heads to protect them from the elements.

events throughout the month of July, involving as many townspeople as possible.

'This is a community hospital in more ways than one,' said the hospital manager, Brian Pressley. 'We serve the community and we are supported by the community'.

WORLD WAR II INTERNMENT

Despite the gathering gloom, the Island was enjoying a successful summer season when war was declared in September 1939.

The British Army, fearful of spies and insurrectionists, began a hurried programme of internment without trial, rounding up thousands of civilians classified as 'enemy aliens'. These included Jews who had fled from Nazi persecution, as well as Germans and Italians who had been living in Britain for many years.

A large and easily secured place to house these people was needed and the Isle of Man was chosen.

Because there was no time for camps to be built, boarding houses were requisitioned. The first properties to be taken over were on Mooragh Promenade, Ramsey. Boarding house keepers were given just six days to vacate their homes, with orders to leave their furniture behind. Many moved in with relatives. The Manx Government undertook to pay them rent and rates and make good any damage.

After a period of intense activity, Mooragh Camp opened on 27th May, 1940 as boatloads of internees began to land at Queen's Pier.

The camp was enclosed by barbed wire and sectioned off internally to prevent different nationalities from intermingling.

At the height of the war, the Island housed 20,000 internees in nine main camps in Ramsey, Peel, Onchan, Douglas and Port Erin.

As the war progressed, many of the internees were allowed to return to the UK mainland.

The war in Europe ended on 8th May 1945 and

During the Second World War the Mooragh Promenade was used to house prisoners. The camp was enclosed by barbed wire and sectioned off internally to prevent different nationalities intermingling. (Manx National Heritage)

Mooragh Camp finally closed on 2nd August that year, so ending a unique period in the town's history.

Work then began on rapidly refurbishing and refurnishing the properties in readiness for the post-war influx of holidaymakers.

Looking south from the internment camp to the Pool Ballroom and the harbour. (Manx National Heritage)

RAMSEY LIFEBOAT

The town of Ramsey began life as a settlement of fishermen's cottages clustered, somewhat precariously, on the shingly sand in the vicinity of today's South Promenade. No wonder then, that it has often been said that Ramsey folk have the sea in their blood.

As a seafaring community, it is somewhat surprising that Ramsey was initially reluctant to accept the RNLI's gift of a 12-oared lifeboat in 1829. Perhaps the expense of maintaining the boat acted as a deterrent. There was also a fatalistic but strongly felt opinion among seafarers that the coasts around Ramsey were unsuitable for rescue vessels. These were probably the reasons why the 1829 boat lay unused in the harbour, exposed to the elements, until it was almost beyond repair.

A fresh start was made in 1868 when the continuous history of Ramsey Lifeboat began.

The *Two Sisters* was the gift of Councillor Ryder of Manchester branch of the RNLI and named after his daughters.

She arrived in November 1868 and was 33ft in length, fitted to pull 10 oars and furnished with a transporting carriage.

Between 40 and 50 seamen volunteered to man the Lifeboat, electing Tom Kaighen as first Coxswain and Robert Fell as second Coxswain. Some of the crew then bore surnames such as Christian, Corkill and Kinnin that have been associated with the lifeboat for generations.

It was not long until the *Two Sisters* rendered good service: on 11th December 1868, she was launched in heavy seas to assist two schooners, the *Jane* from Workington and the *Prudence of Aberystwyth*, that had run aground in a storm in Ramsey Bay, eight lives were saved.

An initial coolness between the well-established Rocket Brigade and the Lifeboat crew soon wore off and the two organisations co-operated in many rescues.

The *Two Sisters* was a good sea boat, but difficult to launch and very hard to row. She was damaged in the great storm of 1st November 1887. In nearly 20 years service, she had saved 147 lives.

Her successor, *Mary Isabella* was the gift of Mr and Mrs J. Norbury, of 'The Carrick', Port Lewaigue, who also provided a new Lifeboat House.

Mary Isabella (2), which followed in 1896, was a very modern and well-equipped boat with the power of righting herself rapidly if capsized. She was responsible for a number of fine rescues and saved 153 lives.

When a barque *Sigrid* got into trouble off Maughold Head in November 1915 it took superhuman efforts to launch the *Mary Isabella* (2). A contemporary report stated:

'The lifeboat was dashed back on to the beach. The crew, in an easterly hurricane, was in imminent danger as the boat was almost standing on end in the breakers. Experienced nautical men assert that the conditions were the worst they had ever known and the lifeboat was in dire peril'.

Fortunately, the crew of the barque were rescued just before their boat was dashed to pieces against the rocks. The lifeboat crew received a special award from the RNLI for gallantry on that occasion.

Ramsey's first motor lifeboat was the *Lady Harrison* (1931 – 1948). Just prior to her arrival, long-serving Coxswain,

The **Mary Isabella** (2) c. 1890 entering the water.

The unusual launch of **Mary Isabella** over the harbour wall in the blizzard of February, 1895, to assist the schooner **Margaret and Elizabeth**.

Crew of **Mary Isabella** (2) (1896-1915). This lifeboat was launched 48 times in that period and saved 153 lives.

John Garrett retired and died soon afterwards. Oscar Corlett also died around that time after 56 years service with the station.

Successive lifeboats and crews have saved many lives at sea, and many honours have been bestowed on crew members for heroism and long service.

In 1895, chairman of the Lifeboat Committee, the Reverend George Paton, said:

'I need not eulogize men whose deeds are their truest eulogy and sufficing glory'. These words still apply today.

The crew are all volunteers and come from all walks of life. The Branch Committee, responsible for administration, and the Ladies' Guild, who do valuable fund raising, also give their time voluntarily. And like all the other RNLI stations, Ramsey's depends on public donations to keep it running.

*Crew of **Mary Isabella** (2) in the late 1890s.*

*Launching the **Mary Isabella** (2) c. 1890, with coxswain Robert Garrett. Hon. Sec. E.C. Kerr is watching the proceedings.*

THE ISLAND'S SCENIC RAILWAY – THE MER

The Manx Electric Railway had its beginnings in 1892 in an enterprise initiated by Frederick Saunderson, an Irish civil engineer who had been living in Ramsey since the late 1860s and who was connected by marriage to the Rowe family of mining engineers.

A railway line, which reached Laxey in May 1894, was constructed by a company that within two years changed its name from the Douglas & Laxey Coast Electric Tramway Ltd. to the Isle of Man Tramways & Electric Power Company Ltd.

Following the success of the Douglas to Laxey line, Ramsey MHK, Mr J.R. Cowell pressed for an extension to Ramsey. This was approved by Tynwald in July 1897 and work began on 1st November.

Work proceeded so rapidly that the line was completed as far as Ballure Station (just south of the railway bridge) in less than a year and was officially opened by the Lieutenant Governor, Lord Henniker on 2nd August, 1898.

A regular and frequent service between Ramsey Ballure and Douglas was provided until the end of October when the line was closed for completion through to the new station adjacent to Ramsey Palace (later re-named the Plaza).

Ballure Railway Bridge was officially opened on 24th July, 1899 and a regular half-hourly service from 7am – 9pm was established. The new railway soon obtained the contract for carrying the mail.

Eighteen months later, the failure of Dumbell's Bank caused the liquidation of the Tramways Company, which was

Car No.20 and saloon trailer No.57 having arrived at Ramsey with the Lieut Governor Sir John Paul and Speaker of the House of Keys Charles Kerruish on the occasion of the re-opening of the line north of Laxey on 25th June 1977.

bought by a Manchester syndicate.

The new company was then given the title Manx Electric Railway Company Ltd. hence 'the MER'.

'Your safe and commodious cars which traverse a piece of the coast, and mountain scenery which suggests the great new road from Sorrento to Amalfi, are, in my view, great contributors to the education and happiness of the thousands who make the Isle of Man their annual resort' – Hall Caine, writing to manager Harold Brown c 1904.

Since 1957 the line has been under the direct control of Tynwald and brings thousands of visitors to Ramsey every summer.

Right: Car No.2, one of the original cars dating from 1893, and one of the tower wagons with the "wire gang" working on the overhead wires behind Waterloo Road in Ramsey. This car and car No.1 are the oldest operating tramcars in regular passenger service in the world but at one time they were used every winter as works maintenance cars. (Stan Basnett)

Below: Winter saloon No.19 and saloon trailer No.57 in Ramsey station. The electric cars are sporting the 1899 livery of the Douglas Laxey & Ramsey Electric that these cars carried when new. (Stan Basnett)

RAMSEY STATION

The first attempt to build a railway from Douglas to Peel was made in 1860 but it was not until April 1870 that agreement was reached in principle to form a railway company to build a line linking Douglas with Peel, Ramsey and Castletown, and later with Port Erin.

The first train to run on the Island from Douglas to Peel was on 1st May 1873; regrettably, one of the locomotives came off the rails at Peel on the first day. Two months later the early initial teething problems of the line were resolved and huge crowds turned out to welcome the new operation. Following the success of the new service, residents in the north of the Island thought that they would be next to get a railway service. Despite the company's initial intentions, it later announced that it had no plans for such an extension. The Northerners decided to go it alone and the Manx Northern Railway Company was formed in 1877 and given government consent in 1878 to build a 16-mile line from St John's to Ramsey, which when built was to become probably one of the most picturesque and scenic lines in the British Isles. The new line was due for completion by 1st July 1879 but not officially opened until 23rd September.

All the railways on the Island continued to blossom through the Victorian and Edwardian periods and up until the Second World War. After the Second World War holidaymakers returned in large numbers: However, with the dawning of package holidays to Spain in the early Sixties, the post-War boom ended in 1956 with over a million passengers being carried for the last time. Costs continued to rise, receipts fell and services started to be reduced.

A loss of £8,000 was made in 1965 and all winter services on the railways were cancelled in order to carry out much-needed maintenance. No trains ran in 1966 but a report to Tynwald on the future of the lines on the Island recognised the importance of the railway services to the community and to visitors. Relief arrived from the Marquis of Ailsa who agreed to lease the lines for 21 years. Hundreds of people turned out in June of the following year on the reopening of the railway operations. However, it was becoming evident that mounting losses were continuing and the decision was made in 1968 to close the St John's to Ramsey line as from 6th September and also to close the Douglas to Peel line the following day. The Peel and Ramsey lines never reopened and eventually the lines and infrastructure was dismantled. Ramsey Station, which was in a poor state of repair at the time of closure, was later demolished and Ramsey Bakery established their new premises.

A view of Ramsey Station shortly after the closure of the St John's line. Today the site is the premises for Ramsey Bakery opposite Shoprite.

Right: This view shows Ramsey Station in July 1963 when the future of the line between St. John's and Ramsey was very much in doubt. Unusually the timetable in this view sees two trains in Ramsey over lunchtime. No 5 Mona is just drawing into the station and No 8 Fenella is already there. The dilapidated state of the buildings is very apparent in this photograph. (Stan Basnett)

Below: Another view of Ramsey Station in the last year of its operation. This picture sees No 5 Mona at the station pending its departure to Kirk Michael and St John's. (Stan Basnett)

MOORAGH PARK

Often described as 'the jewel in Ramsey's crown', Mooragh Park has been a pleasure ground for successive generations since it opened to the public in 1887. An ambitious undertaking from many aspects, it was a fine illustration of foresight and enterprise by our Victorian forebears.

Sheltered on the north and west by brooghs (steep banks), Mooragh Park comprises 40 acres of beautifully landscaped, subtropical gardens enclosing a marine lake with a grassy island at its centre. The lake waters glisten in the sunshine and beyond lies Ramsey Bay and unbroken views to the Cumbrian mountains.

Boats for hire on the lake, a children's playground, water park, competition- standard bowling green, miniature golf, exercise trail, cafes and kiosks are just some of the attractions. In the summer, colourful displays of music and dancing take place on the grass. All year round, the park is used by various sports and leisure groups.

It may come as a surprise to learn that the word mooragh is Manx Gaelic for 'a void place cast up by the sea'.

Prior to 1881, when it was purchased by Ramsey Town Commissioners from the Trustees of the Common Lands (forerunners of the Forestry Division), the Mooragh was a shingly bank, cut off from the town at high tide because a branch of the Sulby River (known as the Old River) flowed on through the present lake and out to sea at the Vollan.

It was a backwater on the edge of the town - a wilderness where only a few fishermen, mushroom gatherers and rabbit hunters ventured.

But the Commissioners saw it as vital to Ramsey's future

Superb panorama of the Mooragh Park and Lake. Note Salt Works chimneys (demolished 1957) in the background.

development as a tourist resort and confidently embarked on a long, difficult, expensive and risky path, which led to the creation of the Mooragh Park we cherish today.

Development of this barren waste ground was set in motion in 1878 when the Reverend William Bell Christian MHK, prompted by the Town Commissioners, and then later moved in Tynwald; that the Trustees for the Commons be authorised to sell the land.

After much debate and negotiation, Tynwald gave its approval and a fair price of £1,200 was agreed. The Deed of Sale was signed in December 1881.

Having completed the purchase, the Commissioners then borrowed £2,000 to allow for improvements.

Architect George Kay was engaged to draw up plans for the transformation of the north part of the bed of the Old River into a Park and Lake.

The plans showed construction of a promenade and sea wall, a swing bridge to link the new promenade with West Quay, and a bridge with sluice gates across the river in North Shore Road. The sluice gates were to allow the Mooragh Lake to be filled and emptied by the tide.

The initial hope was that commodious boarding houses rivalling those on Douglas promenade would be built following construction of North Promenade and the Swing Bridge. But this was impeded by technical problems with construction of the Swing Bridge. It was a debacle that cost the town dearly, as would-be developers who had purchased building plots at highly inflated prices demanded compensation.

The laying out of the park and lake, to the design of Mr E. Thomas, was carried out by Mr F. McCulloch of Manchester for £4,650 and took almost three years to complete. The first gardener was James Corlett, followed by John Martin. After the brooghs (land) were acquired in 1892,

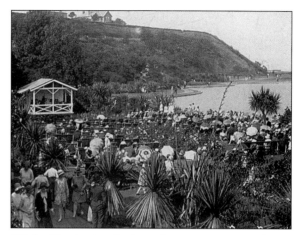

This late-Twenties view takes in an afternoon concert at Mooragh Park.

further planting took place and many townsfolk showed their goodwill by contributing shrubs and trees.

Long years of preparation culminated in the official opening of the Mooragh Estate on August 11th, 1887 by Governor Spencer Walpole. Visitors streamed into the town from all directions for the ceremony. The steamer Tynwald, decked with bunting, arrived from Douglas carrying several hundred passengers. Bands played as they proceeded along streets specially decorated with coloured flags.

His Excellency arrived at Ramsey Railway Station by steam train and was welcomed by chairman of the commissioners, Robert Cowley. At North Promenade, the Governor unveiled a red granite tablet on the sea wall, opposite the end of North Shore Road, where it can still be seen today.

Top: *Edwardian ladies with parasols and gents in boater hats watch rowing races on Mooragh Lake.*

Left: *Sailing boats and rowing boats ready for hire at the boathouse, Mooragh Park.*

Above: *Crown green bowling is still a genteel way to spend a summer's afternoon in Mooragh Park.*

PARLIAMENT STREET

Parliament Street has reflected the social and economic changes of Ramsey for more than a century. As the town's main shopping street, it has seen fortunes made and lost, shopkeepers come and go, trends and fashions arise and fade, buildings go up and come down. It has witnessed murder, fraud, celebration, joy, war, survival, neglect and, most recently, regeneration.

It would take a book in itself to explore the history of Parliament Street, so it may be wise to select a couple of buildings and characters and bring their stories to life.

Arguably one of the most significant buildings in the street is the Saddle Buildings at the southern end, fronting onto Bourne Place. Built around 1880 by Boddington's Hotels on the site of a smithy, Saddle Buildings has a rich history and has often been the subject of heated debate. For example, Saddle Buildings played a vital role during World War II when it was pivotal to the local war effort. One of its roles was as the collecting point for Christmas parcels to be sent to serving soldiers. It was also the headquarters for fundraising efforts such as Warships' Week, when a ladies' committee, aided by the Girl Guides, entreated townspeople to donate aluminium utensils and other articles which could be sold to raise money to build new vessels.

The building was occupied for many years by Holmes' the drapers, then by Looney's general outfitters and in recent years by Felton's ironmongers.

It has come very close to being demolished on several occasions, notably in the early 1980s when it became run down and near derelict. Plans were drawn up to demolish it and replace it with a mock Tudor-style hotel, regardless of the fact that Parliament Street did not even exist in the Tudor period! Fortunately, the plans did not come to fruition.

One of the most fascinating stories of business enterprise in Ramsey surrounds the shop at No. 14 Parliament Street, currently occupied by Costa coffee shop. An imposing building with a warehouse extending to the quay, it was erected in 1887 by an astute business man named Daniel Vondy, owner of the sailing ship *Heather Bell,* which transported corn and seed.

In its time, No. 14 has been many things, including a grocer's and an art gallery. It was also temporary home to Ramsey Town Commissioners at one time.

Interviewed in 1916 after nearly 50 years in business, Daniel Vondy recalled that, when he started out, Parliament Street extended only as far as Clague's Ironmongers (currently Bar Logo).

Among the townsfolk, Parliament Street was regarded as an upmarket destination, usually only visited for the purchase of quality clothing and shoes; most day-to-day items were purchased from shops in 'old' Ramsey, before the area was demolished in the 1960s to make way for the St Paul's Precinct development.

Top: : *Awnings are out so it must be a summer's day, although Parliament Street is unusually quiet. Siesta time perhaps?*

Left: *Ramsey Primitive Methodist Chapel was completed in 1892, but was only used for about fifty years. The site is now occupied by Millichaps' home furnishers.*

Above: *A military band performs at the War Memorial in the Courthouse grounds.*

The Swing Bridge

The 1880s was a period of unprecedented growth for Ramsey, with the creation of Mooragh Park and the laying out of building plots for twenty houses 'of great size' on North Promenade. The plots were quickly snapped up at premium prices, but the success of the investment relied on a bridge being built across the harbour to give access to the town centre.

In September 1888 the contract was awarded to the Cleveland Bridge and Engineering Company, of Darlington. But progress was slow and beset with engineering problems and delays. The bridge was eventually opened, without ceremony, on June 29th, 1892.

The original cost estimate of £8,000 had risen steeply to almost four times that figure and Ramsey ratepayers bore a heavy financial burden for many years after.

The prospect of a yachting marina in the harbour has divided opinion ever since it was first mooted in the 1960s. Although it came very close at one stage, it has yet to become a reality. Throughout the seemingly endless debate, the quayside and harbour remain busy with fishing boats, commercial vessels and pleasure craft – much to the satisfaction of those who

A distinctive study of the swing bridge at Ramsey shortly after its completion. The bridge consists of two pairs of steel trussed arches, each pair spanning 64m to the central pivot point. It is supported at this central point by a circular pier of dressed masonry. The turning mechanism is electrically operated. The main contractor for the bridge was Cleveland Bridge & Engineering Co., Darlington.

Market Place at Ramsey with a variety of interesting coaches and buses waiting to take holidaymakers around the Island during the heyday of the holiday industry.

Another view of Market Place which takes in various market traders, together with the Royal Hotel and the Ship Stores.

This rare view takes in the steam train on the quay loading coal.

65

Left: *A busy scene in Market Place with the Commercial Hotel and steamers in the foreground.*

Above: *Ramsey Quay and Market Place looking towards the Albert Tower on the hill. A variety of buses and coaches are waiting to take passengers around the Island. This view includes the original buildings before the construction of St Pauls Square shopping and homes complex.*

favour its retention as an authentic working harbour.

The steam locomotive (pictured on page 65) is No. 8, *Fenella*, was used to haul wagons loaded with coal along the harbour tramway from the quayside to the goods yard in Station Road.

Work on the track began in the summer of 1892 and the line was first used in December that year. It extended from the goods yard across Bowring Road, then along Derby Road and West Quay.

It was initially used to carry lead ore mined at Foxdale to Ramsey harbour for export. After mining finished in 1911, the main traffic was imported coal, including that for use by the railway itself.

The tramway was last used in 1949. A section at the east end had already been taken out of use in 1924 and the remaining rails were lifted between 1955 and 1957 and the carriageway subsequently resurfaced.

QUEEN'S PIER

The Queen's Pier was built in 1886 to provide a low water landing stage for the increasing numbers of steamers calling at the resort of Ramsey at all levels of the tide. Prior to this, vessels arriving at low tide had to anchor in the bay and wait, often after a long and stormy crossing, adding considerably to the passengers' discomfort.

The plans were prepared by Sir John Goode C.E. and the construction was undertaken by Head Wrightson of Thornaby, England.

Construction began in 1882 and cost more than £45,000. The pier was 2,160ft long (almost half a mile), 20ft wide, and carried on 60 spans. It was illuminated by gas carried on ornamental lamp posts. A tramway ran virtually the whole length.

The formal opening took place on 22nd July, 1886 by Bishop Rowley Hill and, with the gracious consent of Her Majesty, the Lord of Man, Queen Victoria, was christened Queen's Pier. A succession of British monarchs landed at the Pier throughout its history, thus enhancing its 'royal' title.

In its heyday, the Pier saw three return sailings a week between Ramsey and Liverpool, and regular passages between Whitehaven, Workington and Belfast. Smaller pleasure steamers such as the Fairy Queen brought boatloads of passengers from Douglas.

In 1906 around 36,000 passengers used the Pier to get to and from ports in Ireland, England and Scotland. On the pleasure side the Pier provided a venue for angling, swimming, diving demonstrations, band concerts, and evening strolls.

With the outbreak of the First World War, passenger

A rare postcard of Valentino's takes in an afternoon scene from Ramsey Pier with a review of the fleet in the bay of the Royal Navy after the end of the First World War.

numbers dropped and never recovered, as holiday patterns changed and the new, larger ships concentrated on Douglas.

By the late 1960s passenger landings were less than 5,000 and shortly thereafter boats from Belfast and Ardrossan ceased to call at Ramsey at all. The last steamer called in 1970. The Pier remained open to the public with little maintenance until a succession of vandal attacks caused its closure in 1991.

Despite concerted efforts by The Friends of Queen's Pier to have it restored, the future of this elegant structure remains undecided.

Top: *Looking down Ramsey Pier with the railway line. The distinctive row of properties of Stanley Mount East still remain today.*

Left: *Another Keig view shows a pony and trap waiting to take holidaymakers around the Island from the pleasure steamer which has recently arrived.*

Above: *The 'shelter house' at the seaward end of Queen's Pier, where passengers waited to board the vessels.*

A turn of the century view looking from the end of Ramsey Pier towards the town taken by Keig Photographers.

TOURISM AT RAMSEY

A new industry, tourism, emerged in the 1880s when the vogue for seaside holidays, coupled with affordable sea travel, inspired visitors to flock to these shores. While Douglas catered for the working classes, Ramsey established itself as a more genteel resort, with spa hotels such as the Hydro and Dalmeny giving rise to the description 'Queen of Watering Places' in the 1892 Town Guide.

The building boom saw long terraces of tall, elegant lodging houses erected on the North Promenade and Queen's Promenade, and many new hotels sprang up elsewhere. Everybody, it seemed, was taking in visitors.

This new, lucrative industry spurred on the creation of Mooragh Park, along with construction of the Swing Bridge, which was to provide the new houses on North Promenade with easy access to the town.

The Grand Island Hotel

The Grand Island Hotel started life as Beachmount, a mansion built in 1876 for a retired Liverpool sea captain. Neither Mooragh Park nor the Promenade existed and the highway from Bride Road to the shore was just a narrow lane. Beachmount remained a family home until the owner's death in 1894. By then, the visiting industry was beginning to take off and the house attracted the attention of two enterprising gentlemen, Mr J.T. Cowley of Ramsey and Mr E. Roebuck of Cheshire, who planned to capitalise on the recent discovery of underground beds of brine and rock-salt at the Point of Ayre. They bought Beachmount and set about converting it to a

Norman Langford's Manx Mascots entertained audiences at the Cosy Corner on South Promenade in the early 1900s. The tradition started some years earlier when Buxton's Pierrots gave shows twice daily on a stage near the Prince of Wales Hotel.

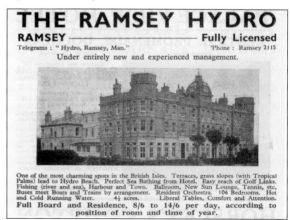

An advertisement taken from the Isle of Man holiday brochure in 1912 of the Ramsey Hydro. Full board and residence was available from 8/6 (43p) to 14/6 (73p) per day according to position of the room and time of the year!

Dancing to well known bands took place every evening except Sundays at the Pool Ballroom & Café .

Another view of the popular Pool Ballroom. Today, the site is used as a parking lot for containers.

The Pool Ballroom on Mooragh Promenade was built adjacent to the open-air swimming baths. It became a great attraction through the war years when dances were held most evenings. Later renamed 'The Talk of the Town' it burned down in the late 1970s.

hotel. It opened as the Ramsey Hydro in the summer of 1897.

After World War One, things were difficult and the business was put in the hands of a receiver and sold to the Hydro (Ramsey) 1926 Ltd. Large building works were carried out, upper floors were added making 54 bedrooms in all, a glass-covered lounge corridor was created on the ground floor and electric lighting was installed. Unfortunately, the cost of these alterations outstripped the company's resources and another receiver was appointed. The new owner was Mr F.G. Whittall of Birmingham. Business continued until 1933 when the Hydro was bought by a company involving members of the Clague family of Port Erin Hydro.

The pre-World War Two era, with its sunny summers, was a time of new investment and optimism. When war broke out, the Hydro was used to billet Territorial Army officers.

The return to peace in 1945 saw a resurgence of tourism and the Hydro resumed its high standing; but by the early 1960s mass tourism was in decline. A new company took over, with the indomitable Helen Lace, formerly of the Fort Anne Hotel, at the helm. With financial support from government, it was transformed into a first class luxury hotel and reopened as The Grand Island Hotel in July 1963.

This company, too, hit financial difficulties and the government intervened by buying the business in 1968 for £150,770. John Marsland, whose catering company was already the tenant, purchased it in 1970 and continued to operate it in association with the Hamilton and Hastings Consortium. Four years later it changed hands again. The new owner was Wilf Blundell, who ran a coach holiday business and filled the hotel with a continuous round of guests. On his sudden death, the family sold to Moiland Investments and Holdings Ltd. who ran it until 1979. The next owner was David Busby from Derby who built up year-round local trade as well as tourism. In 1980, the hotel was busy, but the summer of 1981 was disastrous and led to its closure.

The longest and perhaps most successful chapter began in 1984 with its purchase by John Parkin, daughter Adrienne and son-in-law Trevor Davis. The hotel flourished and was the first in the Island to earn four star status from the AA and RAC and recommendations from Michelin and Egon Ronay.

Financial difficulties combined with Mr Davis' ill-health put it back on the market in 1992 and ultimately into the hands of receivers. Racehorse owner Trevor Hemmings bought it in 1997 and ran it for 12 years, investing at least £350,000 in modernisation.

When the receivers moved in again, staff numbers dropped overnight from 70 to five. A last-minute boost came in the shape of the film industry: Catherine Zeta-Jones, Oliver Tobias, Bill Campbell, James Cromwell, Tony Booth, Anita Dobson and Ray Winstone, who were filming on the Island, were among the famous guests. Eventually, the truth had to be faced: a hotel of this scale and vintage was simply not viable. After 112 years, the doors shut for good on Valentine's Day 2011. The building has since been demolished.

The Ramsey Hydro at the turn of 19th Century.

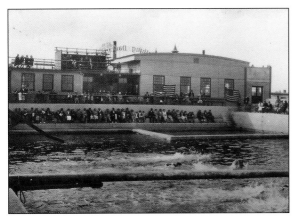

The Pool Ballroom & Café, built in 1935, was as popular with locals as with visitors. Swimming galas and bathing beauty contests were held at the open-air baths during the summer season.

Holidaymakers and residents have always enjoyed the TT. In this view four men of Ramsey with widely differing professions, but with a common interest in the TT view the racing during 1920s.

*Not only was Ramsey visited on a regular basis by the Isle of Man Steam Packet vessels but also excursion vessels from Douglas, Ireland, Scotland and the Lake District visited the port. This view, taken by Keig Photographers, shows most likely the **Manx Fairy** loading passengers.*

RADIO CAROLINE

Ramsey became the epicentre of Sixties' pop culture when the MV *Caroline* dropped anchor three miles out in Ramsey Bay on 6th July, 1964 and Radio Caroline North boomed out across the sea.

Offshore radio, nicknamed 'Pirate Radio', was the brainchild of enigmatic Irishman Ronan O'Rahilly as a reaction to the BBC's staid monopoly of the airwaves.

Employing professional DJs from Britain, USA, Canada and Australia, playing the very latest pop releases and chart hits, the station soon gained millions of listeners and received more than 10,000 fan letters a week.

The public loved the DJs exuberant attitude, which embodied the free spirit of the Sixties. Their frequent mention of 'the sparkling waters of Ramsey Bay' and the 'wonderful Isle of Man', put the Island well and truly on the map in Britain.

Ramsey Steamship Company acted as the ship's agents, providing administration services. Two tenders delivered provisions and ferried ship personnel back and forth. While ashore, crew often stayed at the Commercial Hotel while DJs stayed at The Mitre.

Unsurprisingly, pirate radio ruffled feathers in Whitehall and soon politicians of both main parties were seeking to shut it down. They succeeded when the Marine (Offences) Act became law.

Caroline North fell silent in March 1968, the ship was towed away and was subsequently scrapped.

This chapter in the period of popular culture steadfastly retains a permanent place in the hearts of those lucky enough to have been around during that remarkable era.

A view of Radio Caroline taken by Stan Basnett on the tender run by Ramsey Steamship Company in 1966. (Stan Basnett)

Many local girls made their way out on the tender to Radio Caroline to see the DJs on board and to pass them requests and greetings. (Stan Basnett)

An interesting study of Radio Caroline anchored some three miles off Ramsey taken during the heyday of pirate radio. (Stan Basnett)

THE DARK SIDE

The Mysterious Murder of Betsy Crowe

The death on 20th December, 1888 of Betsy Crowe, remains a mystery to this day. Betsy, a 45-year-old spinster, lived alone in a cottage on the lower slopes of Barrule. She kept two cows and eked out her living by selling milk in Ramsey.

Late one night, just before Christmas, she was returning home, beginning the lonely climb up the Old Douglas Road, when she met her death.

Her body was discovered by a workman early next morning. Her head had been battered by a stone. One of her neighbours, John Henry Gelling was strongly suspected of having committed the crime, but he denied it and was released for lack of evidence.

Years later, a respected local preacher reported that a dying man had confessed to the crime, saying he had been desperate for money and had seen Betsy concealing the milk money in her clothing and had followed her up the lonely track. Despite this revelation, the case was not re-opened and remains unsolved.

The Crown Hotel Murder

Questions which would never be answered remained after the fatal shooting of Ellen Jane Loughran by John Pearson at the Crown Hotel in the summer of 1910. Miss Loughran, 18, was born in Whitehaven, but had spent most of her life in Ramsey. At the time of her death, she was working at the Crown Hotel, Parliament Street as a domestic servant for 18 months and was said to be a quiet, well-mannered girl.

Pearson, 54, had left his home in Yorkshire in 1908 to take

An interesting view of South Ramsey taken from the pier showing Maughold Street.r

on the tenancy of the Crown Hotel. He had previously served in the Army and for a while was posted in India. He was said to have a violent temper and, at times, drank quite heavily. He had a game licence and did some shooting.

At 11.30am on Sunday, 14th August, people heard two shots fired in rapid succession. Police found Miss Loughran lying in the back yard of the hotel, shot in the back of the neck by a double-barrelled shotgun.

Pearson was found upstairs. He had turned the gun on himself and suffered horrific injuries from which he died later that day.

The jury's verdict was that Miss Loughran had died from gunshot wounds inflicted by John Pearson and that he had then committed suicide while of unsound mind. No motive was ever established.

RAMSEY'S FAMOUS SONG

'TWAS once I loved a lass,
I swore I loved her true;
And that I did so long as we
Held Ramsey still in view;
And that I did so long as we
Held Ramsey still in view.

Chorus:
Ramsey Town, 0 Ramsey Town,
Shining by the sea!
Here's a health to my true love,
Wheresoe'er she be.

Her hair was like the gold,
Her eyes, like cloud, were grey.;
We sailed for the blazing South
All on a summer's day. - Chorus.

No grey eyes southward are,
Nor locks of curly gold;
But in the flash of eyes of jet
Lies wealth of love untold. - Chorus.

My heart is not so small
To stop at one, good lack!
I'll love 'em-all, or twenty such,
Grey eyes, or brown, or black!-Chorus.

Homecomers gather in Queen's Hall, Ramsey during the 'The Great Manx Homecoming' of 1927. Organised by Douglas businessman, Arthur Binns Crookall, more than 300 expatriate Manx people who had emigrated to America sailed across the Atlantic to arrive in Douglas Bay to a tumultuous welcome.

Ballure Beach looking north. The row of boarding houses above were later combined as the 90-bedroom Beach Hotel, which boasted a resident orchestra and later, a swimming pool and solarium.

ORIGINS OF THE TOWN & RAMSEY TODAY

Ramsey developed as a town because its bay provides fine natural anchorage. The name, which until the 15th century referred solely to the bay, was given by the Vikings and was first recorded in the Chronicles of Man and the Isles in the 14th century.

Some believe the name 'Ramsey' is derived from the Old Norse 'Hramns-ey' meaning 'Raven's Isle' - a reference to an island at the mouth of the Sulby River - or 'Hramns-a' (Raven's River). Others have suggested 'Rams-a' could be from the Norse for 'wild garlic river', or that it derives from the Norse personal name 'Hramn'.

Ramsey town developed from a small community clustered around the present harbour area. In the early years, fishing was the chief means of survival. It was the dawn of the shipbuilding industry that transformed the town into a busy commercial centre.

A two-year programme got underway in June 2011 to give the town centre a significant makeover. Ramsey Regeneration Committee, chaired by Chief Minister, the Hon. Allan Bell, the town's long-serving MHK, oversaw a joint initiative between government, commissioners and traders to transform the area around the Courthouse into an area that is clean, bright, modern and welcoming. The statue of Godred Crovan and chess partner, located in the Courthouse Grounds, is proving an irresistible subject for photographers.

Ramsey in 2012 underwent a major refurbishment in Parliament Street. This view shows the new Costa café which opened the same year, together with the distinctive figures which have formed part of the modernisation of the street.

An early morning scene taken from the North Breakwater looking towards Ramsey Pier at Maughold Head. (Tom Lloyd-Davies)

A winter scene of Mooragh Park with the early morning sun catching the town and hillside. (Tony Lloyd-Davies)

Above: :An unusual view of Ramsey harbour taken at low water with the fishing boats aground. (Tony Lloyd-Davies)

Left: The Old Courthouse in Ramsey is now used by the Isle of Man Post Office.

Another view of Ramsey Harbour taken at the height of summer with North Barrule in the background. (Tony Lloyd-Davies)

Mooragh Promenade seen as a double image at low water. (Tony Lloyd-Davies)

Looking from the slopes of North Barrule, modern Ramsey can be seen laid out below looking towards the Point of Ayre and Scotland. This view takes in Ramsey Bay Marine Nature Reserve which was established in 2012 following extensive public consultation with a wide range of marine users. A zoning plan protects vulnerable habitats within the bay, notably eelgrass meadows, horse mussel reefs and maerl beds and they are also protected from aggregate extraction and dumping of dredged material. The Conservation Zone (inner bay) is protected from all trawling and dredging and all extraction of scallops and queenies. (Tony Lloyd-Davies)

Ramsey at night reflected in the still waters. (Tony Lloyd-Davies)

Right & Below: Two interesting views of Ramsey Pier captured in the morning sun. The pier opened in 1886 and had a berthing head running at right angles at its seaward end. Steam Packet ships en route to and from Northern Ireland and Scotland called at the pier for passengers staying in the north of the Island. King Edward VII, and later George V, landed on their brief visits to the Island. The pier remains today a Registered Building with uncertain future. (Tony Lloyd-Davies)

Fishing boats and pleasure boats anchored and moored in Ramsey Harbour.
(Tony Lloyd-Davies)

Right: Sprint Day, traditionally held on the Tuesday of TT Race Week, attracts thousands of bikers who swarm in the direction of Mooragh Promenade to watch custom-built bikes reach phenomenal speeds over an eighth of a mile track. On the land side, visitors and locals soak up the fairground atmosphere of fast food stalls, TT memorabilia, stunt displays, vintage motorcycle rally, bouncy castles, carousels and live music. Everything stops at 3pm when the Red Arrows aerobatic team perform death-defying stunts in jet planes above the bay. A different designated official charity each year benefits from bucket collections amongst the crowds. The Sprint has been going for more than 30 years and is a joint venture between the event sponsors and Ramsey Commissioners. (Tony Lloyd-Davies)

Below right: *Another night view of Ramsey Harbour taken by Tony Lloyd-Davies with the Albert Tower floodlit against the backdrop of the dramatic clouds racing across the sky.*